YOUR KNOWLEDGE HAS VALUE

- We will publish your bachelor's and master's thesis, essays and papers

- Your own eBook and book - sold worldwide in all relevant shops

- Earn money with each sale

Upload your text at www.GRIN.com and publish for free

Bibliographic information published by the German National Library:

The German National Library lists this publication in the National Bibliography; detailed bibliographic data are available on the Internet at http://dnb.dnb.de .

This book is copyright material and must not be copied, reproduced, transferred, distributed, leased, licensed or publicly performed or used in any way except as specifically permitted in writing by the publishers, as allowed under the terms and conditions under which it was purchased or as strictly permitted by applicable copyright law. Any unauthorized distribution or use of this text may be a direct infringement of the author s and publisher s rights and those responsible may be liable in law accordingly.

Imprint:

Copyright © 2015 GRIN Verlag, Open Publishing GmbH
Print and binding: Books on Demand GmbH, Norderstedt Germany
ISBN: 9783668370944

This book at GRIN:

http://www.grin.com/en/e-book/350574/achieving-human-rights-compliance-in-drone-operations

Anna Scheithauer

Achieving Human Rights Compliance in Drone Operations

A Case for the Human Rights Council's Special Procedures (HRCSP)

GRIN Publishing

GRIN - Your knowledge has value

Since its foundation in 1998, GRIN has specialized in publishing academic texts by students, college teachers and other academics as e-book and printed book. The website www.grin.com is an ideal platform for presenting term papers, final papers, scientific essays, dissertations and specialist books.

Visit us on the internet:

http://www.grin.com/

http://www.facebook.com/grincom

http://www.twitter.com/grin_com

Achieving Human Rights Compliance in Drone Operations: A Case for the Human Rights Council's Special Procedures (HRCSP)

In this essay I will argue that the added-value of the HRCSP lies in the special rapporteurs' (SR) role as *facilitators* for norm compliance. Doing so, I will focus on the post-9/11 debate on the use of armed drones for targeted killings in military and counter-terrorism operations. Its main point of contention surrounds the achievement of consistency in legal standards, as well as of coherent policy responses with view to the "war on terror", which has led some states to prioritize security concerns over human rights (HR) and humanitarian standards.

In presenting my argument I will make reference to actor behavior theory to show the nexus between HRCSP and strategic agency. Thereby, I shall concentrate on mechanisms of social influence such as coercion, persuasion, incentives, and capacity building as identified by Risse and Popp (R&P). (2013, 12-22) Also, I will address the element of acculturation, found as a major force for compliance by Goodmann and Jinks (G&J) (2004), and touch on domestic mechanisms, such as executive power, litigation, and group demands (Simmons, 2009), and the power of domestic constituencies (Dai, 2004). During the analysis, I will be mindful of a possible crowding-out effect as suggested by G&J, where one social mechanism could negatively affect the operation of another. (2013, 105)

In this sense I will elaborate on the opportunities and challenges of the HRCSP regarding compliance with the right to life in human rights law (HRL) and humanitarian law (IHL) with view to targeted killings. I will focus on the HRCSP because they embody the permanent tools of the Human Rights Council (HRC) composed of independent experts, compared to the Universal Periodic Review (UPR), which, due to its politicized nature, is rather silent on the subject matter. The analysis will show how the Special Rapporteur for Extrajudicial, Summary and Arbitrary Executions (SRESAE) and the Special Rapporteur on Terrorism and Human Rights (SRTHR), in concerted action and by application of various elements of socialization, facilitate the compliance process.

First, they do so by facilitating the process of institutionalizing norms (G&J, 2004), through standard setting, interpretation and elaboration. This is evidenced by the scope of their mandate and the endorsement of their reports by the HRC and other treaty bodies. (Abresh et al., 2008, 195-197) This interactive process aiming for norm clarity provides potential in that it might offset the "crowding-out effect" brought about by scrutinizing norm violating countries, which often leads them to interpret their legal obligations rather differently. (Clark, 2013, 144)

Second, they facilitate the discursive socialization process through a) monitoring and fact-finding, b) inviting for dialogue, and c) conferring with civil society organizations. Empowering victims through individual petitions might threaten states into compliance. (Clark, 2013) But coercion might be less effective when it comes to public procedures since states tend to conceal information as low response rates to communications suggest. (G&J, 2004) Despite country responses being mostly based on national priorities, this might reflect an opportunity for a more consultancy-oriented approach (Limon and Piccone (L&P), 2014, 25) and encourage follow-up, the weakest link by far. In terms of dialogues, strategic positioning seems the rule. This is evidenced by voting behavior and positions adopted during HRC debates. (UNOG (1), 2014). Nevertheless, the "contagion effect" - countries adopting the position of allies or regional partners – is suggested to hold equal potential for counter-hegemonic and pro-hegemonic norm diffusion. (G&J, 2004, 653) Finally, civil society organizations exposing governments' misconduct constitute a valuable source of information for the SR. The adoption of soft law instruments by the US exemplifies the importance of "naming and shaming" by civil society actors, and domestic regimes for compliance with authoritative decisions. (Simmons, 1998, 78)

I will conclude that the SR are not an end but a means for achieving compliance. There is also no one solution regarding the socialization process, which seems to strongly depend on the right sequencing of elements sensitive to certain scope conditions and the level, or "continuum of commitment" (Dai, 2013, 86-87), states prescribe themselves to depending often on domestic mechanisms of influence. Hence, a lack of cooperation shouldn't bring doubt about the SR nor lead to their discontinuation. It is in this face of strategic agency that the post-9/11 discourse calls for independent experts with strong mandates.

HRCSP: Facilitators for Norm Compliance

Targeted killings reached their peak in 2010, and by 2013 more than fifty countries were already reported to have drone capabilities. (ICRJ, 2013) This makes the need for compliance with the provisions on the right to life in the ICCPR and Geneva Conventions apparent. However, states' policy responses reflect the "war on terror" and diverge widely. In this respect actor behavior theory helps to explain states' conduct and sheds light on mechanisms of social influence the SR can employ to facilitate compliance with these conflicting norms. Here it is to mention that international relations theories acknowledge all these mechanisms. Variation lies merely in the ontological emphasis they put on them (G&J, 2004, 630-632). Such discussion is though beyond the scope of this paper.

Various approaches have been developed to explain the paradox of state compliance with non-reciprocal HR treaties lacking enforcement power. (G&J, 2004, 628-629) Amongst the scholarly literature, R&P identified four socialization mechanisms to direct states towards compliance: coercion, persuasion, incentives, and capacity building, each featuring various "modes of social action" such as i.e. sanctions & rewards, naming & shaming, discursive power, and institution-building. These mechanisms dependent on scope conditions such as regime type, consolidated/limited statehood, centralized/decentralized rule implementation, and material and social vulnerability. (2013, 12-22) Compliance is said to be higher i.e. in democratic than authoritarian countries suggesting that mechanisms like persuasion and naming & shaming will be more successful with the former and incentives with the latter.

However, when it comes to the level of commitment findings contradict this view: Hathaway shows that democracies with poor HR records are less likely to commit because treaties will lead to real changes in behavior, while countries with less democratic institutions are more likely to commit due to slim prospects of enforcement (2007). Moreover, Simmons points to democratic countries like the US, which are in principle committed but fail to ratify ("false positives") and concludes in line with Moravcsik (2000) that transitional regimes bear most commitment potential. (2009, 58, 153) This affects the interaction between mechanisms and scope conditions and needs to be born in mind for the subsequent analysis.

Furthermore, G&J stress acculturation as a distinct social mechanism based on social and cognitive pressures, whereby states tend to assimilate upon assessment of their social relations rather than due to norm internalization or imposition of material sanctions. (2004, 639-643)

Also, and most importantly G&J caution against a possible "crowding-out effect" of social mechanisms, finding that material and social incentives are often incompatible, and stress the importance of sequencing. (2013, 106;116) Finally, with view to the domestic level, Dai argues that HR treaties empower domestic constituencies, which in turn effect compliance (2005), while Simmons points to elite agenda-setting, litigation, and political mobilization as the main channels of influence. (Simmons, 2009) However, she thereby neglects to address how meaningful and possible these channels are. (Scheithauer, 2013)

In this sense, actor behavior theory suggests, among challenges, potential for the SR, which are vested with the strongest mandates among the HRCSP (L&P, 2014, 15), to facilitate the compliance process. First, they do so by facilitating the process of institutionalizing norms (G&J, 2004), through standard setting, interpretation and elaboration.

Within the debate on drone operations, major discussions on compliance between the SR and member states relate to conflicting interpretations of the law. For example, the US maintain that the HRC and HRCSP lack competence to deal with targeted killings carried out in the name of the "war on terror". As she is in a state of war with terrorist suspects, IHL is applicable to the exclusion of HRL, which falls outside the scope of the SR mandate. (Abresh et al., 2008, 186) The UK holds a similar position concluding that the HRC is "[...] not the appropriate forum to discuss weapons on a thematic basis [...]" (UNOG (1), 2014) This fits with Clark's assumption of countries exhibiting defensive behavior upon scrutiny starting to engage in different interpretations of their obligations. (2013, 144) But it also provides an example not corresponding to R&P's finding on democratic regimes; nor can the US and UK be classified as "false positives" in Simmon's sense. Nevertheless, we can agree with G&J that the applicability of social sanctions is questionable in this case. Such measure would require higher legal precision to be considered legitimate by sponsoring and targeted states. (2004, 684)

However, communications by the SR can be considered a valuable tool not only for bringing violations to attention, but also to elaborate on such standards and procedures. As stipulated in communications between the US and the SRESAE (Abresh et al., 2008), ECOSOC Res. 1235 (XLII) establishing the HRCSP requires thematic procedures to consider HR violations in all countries without limitation to particular treaties. (L&P, 2014, 7) The same goes for the SRESAE's mandate, being defined by a phenomenon rather than a legal regime. (SRESAE Handbook, 2004-2010, 6). As to the complementarity of HRL and IHL, this is stipulated in the HRC's Institution Building Resolution 5/1 (para.2) and was affirmed multiple times by the HRC endorsing the reports of the SR reflecting the affirmative views of various treaty and judicial bodies on this matter. (Abresh et al., 2008, 195-197)

Time will tell if such interaction between the SR and governments, as well as other treaty bodies can counteract the crowding-out effect scrutiny brings about. So far, it has still allowed the SR to proceed progressively: i.e. drones were first taken up by the SRESAE in 2002/3 regarding Yemen (O'Connell, 2010, 3) reflecting the organic evolution of the SP' mandate driven by states' demands to react to new and changing circumstances. (Abresh et al., 2008, 202-203) The endorsement of the SR' reports over the last decade led among others to the adoption of HRC Res. 25/22, GA Res. 68/178 and the decision to convene a panel discussion on the subject. Even though resolutions aren't binding they embody a decisive acculturation tool for the establishment of durable norms. (G&J, 2004, 689) Nevertheless, the challenge remains getting member states to make meaningful use of such soft law instruments during the UPR. (Kälin, 2013, 456)

Second, SR facilitate the discursive socialization process. Monitoring and fact-finding via communications and country visits prove valuable activities. Thematic mandates are well-equipped to holistically address topics otherwise left unexamined by shuttling between headquarters and the field. (Hoehne, 2007) Clark finds in her study on the UN Convention Against Torture (CAT) that individual petitions by empowering victims threaten states into compliance as they signalize potential domestic audience costs. (2013) However, petitions are a long and cumbersome process embodying an ex-post mechanism hindering the SR to respond rapidly to targeted killings. In this sense, the SR enjoy limited early warning possibilities as targeted killings are hardly known in advance (Nifosi, 2005 97). Also, contradictory to Clark's finding, G&J suggest that for non-compliant states petitions might simply signal a potential fine to be paid for violations of their obligations. Particularly with view to the post-9/11 debate this risks justice being equated with compensation "incentivizing" states to ignore their reporting obligations when faced with material sanctions. (2013, 115-116)

As statistics (2013) show, response rates to SRTHR and SRESAE communications are one of the lowest with 43% and 46% (L&P, 2014, 30). Besides agency-related challenges this is also due to resource constraints as states are often overwhelmed with the increase in mandates.

(Hoehne, 2007, 11) In either case, joint communications could reduce the amount of duplicate responses, and convey stricter urgency. Moreover, a report by the Universal Rights Group states that country responses are mostly based on national priorities. Critics maintain this would turn the SP into a HR consultancy, which is what some states have been trying to promote. But rather to dismiss the idea entirely, it could serve beneficial under the capacity building mechanism and a working group on armed drones could be established for this purpose. This might also encourage follow-up, which has remained the weakest link featuring an ill-equipped HRCSP toolbox with a Code of Conduct silent on this matter. (L&P, 2014, 10; 25)

Furthermore, the complementarity of thematic and country mandates stressed at the Vienna Conference provides opportunities for dealing with armed drones more systematically. (L&P, 2014, 8) The 21st Special Session on Israel on the HR situation in the Occupied Palestinian Territory addressing the (thematic) issue of drones exemplifies this. (UNOG (2), 2014) Even though member states have accused the HRC for its politicized nature and selectivity, this doesn't necessarily hold true for the work of the SP. (Hoehne, 2007, 10) In fact, the HRC proves an important forum for the SP to engage in dialogue with member states, and it is also in this sense that the SP facilitate the discursive socialization process.

Through Interactive dialogues mandate-holders present their reports in a cluster upon which member states deliver their statements. But as time constraints don't allow to address all comments and questions it leaves to wonder how interactive and dialogical these debates are. (L&P, 2014, 31) Nevertheless, progress can be noticed with view to the decision to convene a panel discussion dedicated specifically to armed drones. The statements presented during the debate show the strategic positioning of states (UNOG (1), 2014), which is also reflected by the voting behavior on HRC Res. 25/22 on the same subject. For example, the US, UK and France opposed the resolution, while a large number of US allies such as Germany, Italy and Austria abstained, as did most NATO countries. Other powerful opposition countries like China and Russia voted in favor, followed by i.e. Pakistan, the resolution's main sponsor and a country strongly affected by drone operations. (2014, 3) This "contagion effect" is said to hold equal potential for the diffusion of counter-hegemonic norms as it does for pro-hegemonic ones. (G&J, 2004, 653) Adoption of HRC Res. 25/22 despite hegemonic opposition illustrates this point and is expression of the acculturation mechanism at work.

A final way for the SP to facilitate the discursive socialization process is by conferring with civil society organizations. The HRCSP are a focal point not only for governments but NGOs and the media alike. The SREASE and SRTHR are the strongest HRCSP in media representation (L&P, 2014, 33) benefitting from it by increased access to information and influence on domestic factors. As Simmons puts it, the normative power of international standards legitimizes holding governments to account. (1998, 88) Hence, when combined with the "power of visibility" through "naming and shaming" change in actor behavior is predictable. (G&J, 2004, page) Dai employing a game theoretical model in her study shows that states' motivations for compliance largely depends on the electoral leverage and informational status of domestic constituencies. (2005) When combining this finding with Simmons domestic mechanisms one can see why public scrutiny by i.e. Human Rights Watch during HRC debates, the issuance of joint letters (HRW, 2014) and dual reports, as well as joint press releases (Rawling, 2013) on armed drones triggers state response.

The adoption of soft law instruments such as the "U.S. Policy Standards and Procedures for the Use of Force in Counterterrorism Operations Outside the United States and Areas of Active Hostilities" (Whitehouse, 2013) or the "No strike and the collateral damage estimation methodology" (Chairman of the joint chiefs of staff instruction, 2012) by the US exemplify the importance of civil society actors and domestic regimes for "second order compliance" - compliance with authoritative decisions - (Fisher in Simmons, 1998, 78) though they are not without critique. Regulations are still half-hearted, which suggests that domestic audience costs in the face of the "war on terror" aren't yet high enough. Thus, it remains questionable whether any of the four domestic mechanisms can hold here what theory suggests.

Conclusion

The analysis has shed light on the opportunities and challenges the HRCSP face in confrontation with member states' strategic agency. The post-9/11 agenda has in this sense produced a powerful counter-discourse, and with it a lack of compliance with standards on the right to life, as to targeted killings via armed drones. We have come to see that the SREASE and SRTHR are not an end in themselves but rather a means for achieving compliance by facilitating the socialization process. Thereby, the SR can draw from the various actor behavior theories on social and domestic mechanisms of influence as guidance for the appropriate employment of their tools.

As the analysis has shown, caution is to be exercised with view to identifying the right combination and sequence of mechanisms. This often depends, but as shown could also fall short of, the stated scope conditions. Moreover, it has become clear, that states usually comply somewhat with their obligations rather than completely or not at all. This points to a "continuum of commitment" (Dai, 2013) requiring the reconciliation of the mechanisms also with states' level of commitment. In this sense, it is precisely because of a lack of state cooperation that the value of the HRCSP and the need for strongly mandated SR in the post-9/11 era have become apparent.

Bibliography

Abresh, William; Alston, Philip; Morgan-Foster, Jason; (2008) "The Competence of the UN Human Rights Council and its Special Procedures in relation to Armed Conflicts: Extrajudicial Executions in the ' War on Terror '", The European Journal of International Law Vol. 19 No. 1, pp. 183–209

Chairman of the joint chiefs of staff instruction (2012) "No strike and the collateral damage estimation methodology", CJCSI 3160.01A, last accessed: 6 March 2015 https://info.publicintelligence.net/CJCS-CollateralDamage.pdf

Clark, Ann Marie (2013) "The Normative Context of Human Rights Criticismm: Treaty Ratification and UN Mechanisms" Risse, Thomas; Ropp, Stephen; Sikking, Kathryn (2013) The Persistent Power of Human Rights: Form Commitment to Compliance, UK: Cambridge University Press, pp. 125-144

Dai, Xinyuan (2005) "Why Comply? The Domestic Constituency Mechanism", International Organization, Vol. 59, No. 2, pp 363 - 398

Dai, Xinyuan (2013) "The "Compliance Gap" and the Efficacy of International Human Rights Institutions", Risse, Thomas; Ropp, Stephen; Sikking, Kathryn (2013) The Persistent Power of Human Rights: Form Commitment to Compliance, UK: Cambridge University Press, pp. 85-102

UN General Assembly, Human Rights Council: Resolution "5/1. Institution-building of the United Nations Human Rights Council" / adopted by the General Assembly, 7 August 2007, A/HRC/RES/5/1

UN General Assembly, Human Rights Council : Resolution "Ensuring use of remotely piloted aircraft or armed drones in counter-terrorism and military operations in accordance with international law, including international human rights and humanitarian law" / adopted by the General Assembly, 24 March 2014, A/HRC/25/L.32

Goodman, Ryan and Jinks, Derek (2013) "Social Mechanisms to Promote International Human Rights: Complementary or Contradictory?", Risse, Thomas; Ropp, Stephen; Sikking, Kathryn (2013) The Persistent Power of Human Rights: Form Commitment to Compliance, UK: Cambridge University Press, pp. 103-122

Hathaway, Oona (2007) "Why Do Countries Commit to Human Rights Treaties?", The Journal of Conflict Resolution, Vol. 51, No. 4, Sage Publications, Inc. pp. 588-621

Hoehne, Oliver (2007) "Special Procedures and the New Human Rights Council – A Need for Strategic Positioning", Essex Human Rights Review, Vol. 4, No. 1, last accessed: 6 March 2015, http://projects.essex.ac.uk/ehrr/V4N1/Hoehne.pdf

Human Rights Watch (2014) "Joint Letter to the UN Human Rights Council on Targeted Killings and the Use of Armed Drones", last accessed: 6 March 2015 http://www.hrw.org/news/2014/09/18/joint-letter-un-human-rights-council-targeted-killings-and-use-armed-drones

International Justice Resource Centre (ICRJ) (2013) "UN Special Rapporteur Initiates Investigation into Drone Strikes and Other Targeted Killings", last accessed: 6 March 2015 http://www.ijrchenter.org/2013/02/04/un-special-rapporteur-initiates-investigation-into-drone-strikes-and-other-targeted-killings/

Kälin, Walter (2013) "Universal Human Rights Bodies and Promoting Humanitarian Law", Kolb, Robert and Gaggioli, Gloria (2013) Research Handbook on Human Rights and Humanitarian Law, Edward Elgar Publishing: Cheltenham/UK

Limon, Marc, and Piccone, Ted (2014) "Policy Report: Human Rights Special Procedures: Determinants of Influence - Understanding and Strengthening the Effectiveness of the UN's Independent Human Rights Experts", Universal Rights Group

Moravcsik, Andrew (2000) "The Origins of Human Rights Regimes: Democratic Delegation in Postwar Europe", International Organization, Vol. 54, No. 2, The MIT Press, pp. 217-252

O'Connell, Mary Ellen (2010) "Unlawful Killing with Combat Drones: A Case Study of Pakistan, 2004-2009", Notre Dame Law School, Legal Studies Research Paper, No. 09-43

Rawling, Nate (2013) "Amnesty International and Human Rights Watch Blast US Drone Strikes: New Reports From Amnesty International and Human Rights Watch Challenge The Legality of U.S. Drone Strikes in Pakistan and Yemen", Time, http://world.time.com/2013/10/22/amnesty-international-and-human-rights-watch-blast-u-s-drone-strikes/

Risse, Thomas and Ropp, Stephen (2013) "Introduction and Overview", Risse, Thomas; Ropp, Stephen; Sikking, Kathryn (2013) The Persistent Power of Human Rights: Form Commitment to Compliance, UK: Cambridge University Press, pp. 3-26

Ryan Goodman and Derek Jinks (2004) How to influence states: Socialization and International Human Rights Law, Duke Law Journal, Vol. 54, No. 3, p. 621-703

Scheithauer, Anna (2015) "Human Rights Treaty Commitment and Compliance", Seminar Notes, Human Rights Standards and Institutions, UCL, London, 3rd March 2015

Simmons, Beth (1998) "Compliance with International Agreements", Annual Review of Political Science, Vol. 1, pp. 75-93

Simmons, Beth (2009) Mobilizing for Human Rights: International Law in Domestic Politics, New York: Cambridge University Press

UNOG (1) – United Nations Office in Geneva (2014), "Human Rights Council holds Panel on Remotely Piloted Aircraft or Armed Drones in Counterterrorism and Military Operations", last accessed: 6 March 2015
http://www.unog.ch/unog/website/news_media.nsf/%28httpPages%29/BCE56ED914A46D40C1257D5B0038393F?OpenDocument

UNOG (2) – United Nations Office in Geneva (2014) "Human Rights Council Opens Special Session on the Human Rights Situation in the Occupied Palestinian Territory", last accessed: 6 March 2015
http://www.unog.ch/80256EDD006B9C2E/%28httpNewsByYear_en%29/4C9CDF7FE83E0581C1257D1E00434418?OpenDocument

UN Special Rapporteur on Extrajudicial Executions Handbook (2004-2010), The Project on Extra Judicial Executions, Center for Human Rights and Global Justice, New York University School of Law, last accessed: 6 March 2015
http://www.extrajudicialexecutions.org/LegalObservations%3FopenCategory=0.html

Whitehouse (2013) U.S. Policy Standards and Procedures for the Use of Force in Counterterrorism Operations Outside the United States and Areas of Active Hostilities, last accessed: 6 March 2015
http://www.whitehouse.gov/sites/default/files/uploads/2013.05.23_fact_sheet_on_ppg.pdf

YOUR KNOWLEDGE HAS VALUE

- We will publish your bachelor's and master's thesis, essays and papers

- Your own eBook and book - sold worldwide in all relevant shops

- Earn money with each sale

Upload your text at www.GRIN.com
and publish for free